Why So Many !?

Compiled By :
Heart's Database & Team

Copyright © 2020 by **Famian**

All rights reserved.
"Why Should I Marry"

Published by **FAMIAN**

No part of this publication may be reproduced, distributed or transmitted in any form or by any means including photocopying, recording or any other electronic or mechanical methods without the prior written document of the publisher, except in the case of brief quotations embodied in critical reviews and certain other non-commercial uses permitted by copyright law.

For permission requests, write to the publisher, addressed.
"Attention: Permissions Co-ordinator" at our mail,

Email:
famian.onl9@gmail.com

DISCLAIMER

This book is a collection of real thoughts and opinion stories. Names, characters, places, and incidents either are the product of the author(s) real lives or are used in a fictitious manner.

CATALOGING-IN-PUBLICATION DATA

Title: Why Should I Marry?

Compiler: Heart's Database & Team

Book Type: Stories and Quotes

Genre: Self Help

Published by: Famian

Concept by: Kamlesh Mishra

Cover Design by: Amey Wadegaonkar

Content Support By: Kayathri Kumar, Lalitha Priyadharshini ,Shaik Sajida and Geethanjali A.

Edited by: Umme Haani

Proof Read by: Kinjal Khanna, Sakshi Tekade, Panchanand Gupta and Tritrishna Ghosh

Managed By: Alpesh Chandora

Supported by: Keval Suchak, Syed Faiz Ibrahim and Arshiya Patel

SPONSORED BY

ACKNOWLEDGEMENT

First and foremost, praises and thanks to the God, the Almighty, for his showers of blessings throughout the course of our work for this book.

We express our sincere gratitude to our sponsors **Pro Rich, B.S.R A.S.A Diary 786, JK Parker Mixer Grinders, Taqdees Assortments, A&M Fashions** and **Pen and Laptops** for their contribution and support. We are thankful to each co-author associated with this book for their active participation.

We are indebted to **Umra Ahmed** and **Sagar Chavan** for their content and support.A Special thanks to each of our FAMIAN team members for their constant and time-to-time support. Without them and their co-operation, completion of this book would have been difficult and their presence was totally indispensable.

CONTENTS

INTRODUCTION

Marriage! But why? The one question we all had at some point of life, it might be a choice of love for some while for others it might be compulsion by law. It is a speculative question which never crossed the minds of our antecedents but, it is a question which never leaves the minds of today's young crew. We all have wondered about the need for marriage and might have even discussed. The question arises when there is a clash between an individual's self sufficiency and a craving for mutual dependence.

Marriage is a journey which takes us through a huge tunnel of transitions. Though it is seen as a bond that unites two families rather than just a bond of two souls, digging into the topic further; the opinions seem quite simple or damn silly. The idea of marriage takes shape right from the moment a human begins to understand their fellow neighbours. The society adds much more ingredient to better understanding. Directly or indirectly we're pulled into the maze of marital institution. Not every question gives you a definite answer some questions make you think, venture yourself and even make you do a reality check on yourself. More than practical validations one needs an emotional, psychological acceptance of the people they're going to hold lifelong. So, why not the individual decide what he or she needs than someone or society programming and scheduling the things or people they need in their phases of life. Unlike other relations, a marital companion needs to accompany you through hell and heaven of life's roller-coaster ride. So, it's better to take a reality check before tightening your seat belts for the ride.

Marriage may be a bond created by love or a bond that creates love. Some say that the sacred thread does magic in binding two souls while some others argue that if love binds the souls, there is no need for a sacred rope. Either way, some people are eager to face the adventure and others fear at the risk of getting trapped. When a proposal knocks at your doorstep guaranteeing a life-time care, a shoulder to lean on, a promising life, whatsoever; what would be your answer?

What's your move on the question, would you nod a yes or strike a No. Whatever the answer is, it solely depends on the interest of the person and not the question bearer.

This book will let you hear out the opinions of him/her who ones had a thought like you.

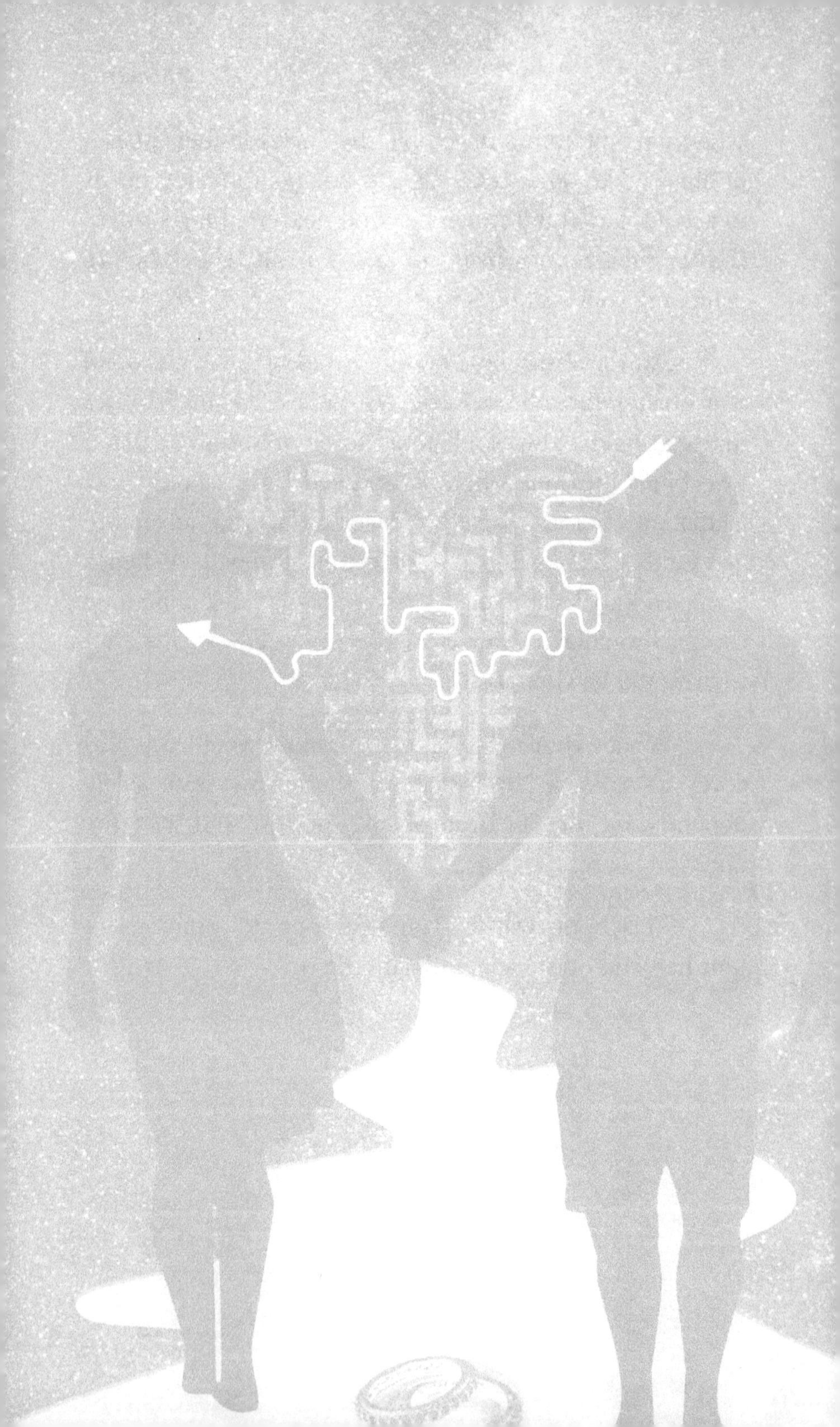

TWIRLED LIFE

By: Neha Nandwani

In the extreme corner of the class, just where the walls limit the classroom, in the kingdom of the backbenchers, I was sitting with few of my friends, having some girly talks with them. She was me, telling my friends that I will marry that boy sitting on the 3rd bench of the second row. But later on, classes changed, school changed, thoughts changed and I came to know that it was all childish. It is the age which makes you think like that.

Then I was in junior college, Its obvious that you go to college for not only studying but also doing fun with mates. But seriously speaking, I never bunk any of my class. I was the regular type and had no fun in college. No no, I am not from the'90s but can't help as my college was too strict. At the end of 10+1, I finally decided to change my college with a thought 'Is this a college? Where there is no fun, no *gapshap* nothing, so boring!'

Oh yes! I finally changed my college. There I came to know what college life is! Roaming with girls and boys I found peace, in the corner over there watching couples having romantic talks, found boring until a boy came into my life, not with a question, 'Will You Marry Me?' but with a question, 'Do you have any boyfriend?' Obviously, at that time I was single but still, I was confused about what to reply as a friend of mine once told me that even if you are single tell them you are mingle. But as it was my first time I thought let's try how it is! So I replied to him, "No, I don't have any boyfriend yet!" And from there the whole drama began...

After completion of junior college, he moved to Pune for further studies. It was a quite good simple type of long- distance relationship. We both enjoyed each other's company and thought to enjoy it lifetime. Three years passed, graduation got completed but this time thoughts did not change; they were same as before, to marry the same guy. After one month, we were having good jobs, we became well settled and completely matured. I must say qualified for marriage. Yeah! that's the sad truth of our society that you need to be well studied, well earned, well-matured to do *'SHUBH MANGAL SWAHA !'*

And here the question that every girl is waiting to hear came from him, "Will You Marry Me?" I was super excited to say YES. But I don't know what happened to me and I replied, "NO" full stop. That two minutes of silence occurred. We both went completely silent. I didn't understand myself when I was so excited for it then why did I reply No? It was the big twist of my life that even I was not able to understand myself . He poorly went back with a saddened heart. After that, neither had he tried to contact me nor did I. When I thought with a calm mind that why did I reject him I got to know that I was not ready for all that wedding formalities. I needed some time for myself, for my career.

So, I decided to build up my career first and then to find a life partner. I started moving on doing hard work but again then what obstructed me was *'Beta ab tumhe shadi kar leni chahiye!'* At the age of 22, my family forcefully started finding me a perfect husband. Although I was not interested in arrange marriage, I had to go along with my family each next day to see some other boy. I got completely frustrated and one day I said, "*Mujhe Shadi Hi Nahi Karni!*" And over there whole drama stopped.

Now, I am 28. I am a versatile artist, self-confident and an independent type of girl. Today, I have my own business, self-made home and decent savings, but still, I am feeling incomplete. And now I am thinking *'Kya Ab Mujhe Shadi Kar Leni Chahiye?'* I am completely ready for the wedding. But over there I am thinking, 'Didn't I Pass the Right Age For Marriage?' Is there any right age to marry someone? Or Is there any perfect boy left for me at the age of 28? Or should I have left my career and would have married my love? Now, do I need to do any compromises with my life? Will I get a guy that meets my expectation? Until then I am waiting for that one guy who is made for me!

In the last, I would just like to say that, " *SHAADI EK AISA FAL HAI JO KHAYE PACHTAYE, JO NAA KHAYE WO BHI PACHTAYE !*" which means marriage is like that fruit if you eat it then you will regret, and if you don't eat then too you will regret.

*****

"Marriage isn't about getting tied together! It's all about the love you tied around and the hatred you burnt there around the fire!"

- **Yashvi Srivastava**

FAIRYTALE

By: Drishti Sharma

The connotation 'she lives in the fairytale' literally describes me in the best humanly possible way. I am a girl who lives in fairytale,. Yes that's what every person who knows me calls me. I am the person who sees this world a little different, who thinks there is always something to bring a bright smile on a face. You can think of me as Madhuri Dixit of "*Dil toh pagal hain*" or Geet of "Jab we met".

I am 22, and somehow from this age talks of marriage comes. Marriage and love are such a pure thing for me like it's the most beautiful thing that can happen to someone. To spend your whole life with someone, loving and caring for them and see their smile which will be worth everything. From my high school days, I have seen many friends in love and promising each other marriage but every time they broke up and cry it was like a slap on my fairytale idea like "Ouch, it was not supposed to be like that". I got scared to love, to stop my fairytale to end in heartbreak because for me love comes before marriage. Every time I got feelings for someone, I leave them before they leave me because I want to end my love with marriage and I think "Nah , this world will not understand me" and leave that feeling gracefully.

I started focusing on my career and dreamt of working in a well-known multinational company and to my luck, I got that dream job. I had always wanted to do something so that the world knows me by my name. Oh! Did I forget to mention I just love my name so much? But to my surprise, I came to know that in my culture there is a ritual to change the first name along with the last name after marriage, "Oops, means marriage not only is gonna change my life but my identity too. No one is gonna know that name which I want to be known by to every person".

Reality does hit hard. I slowly started accepting the reality that that's how life is supposed to be but always a question pops up " Is it worth to lose yourself whole as a person , to change your identity for someone , what if he never gets my point of view of life, what if he never saw that spark in my eyes when I talk about or work on my dreams". For me, marriage is the happiness of not only two individuals but also of two families and are we gonna be two happy families? These questions do scare me as I want to love someone fully but, in the process, don't want to lose myself as a person, that's what makes me different.

I know, in reality, fairytales don't exist and somehow we have to adjust or compromise, but still, I am waiting for someone who will understand my fairytale world and live with me in it and the day I will find him I will say a big "Yes". Till then, I am going to live in my fairytale with some reality checks because I know that dreams do come true and someone will be worth every risk and there will be no doubts and we will be imperfectly perfect.

*****

"Marriage is a journey of commitment to growing old with each other, accepting each other's imperfections as a habit of own with love"

- Nirali U. Potdar

BLESSINGS

By: Anusha L.

Just like any other family with orthodox mindset, I grew up in a family where talking to anyone from the opposite gender apart from my family members was against the sacraments any Indian girl was taught by their family. I just want to share my story about marriage. Going through my life journey, I struggled a lot to find out the exact meaning for "Why we marry?". From my childhood, my father was very much strict with me. He always warns me to not to speak with the opposite gender because he was very much frightened for me. He wanted me to become a disciplined girl. So, when I see the opposite gender, automatically fear comes to my mind and I avoid them. Because I don't know, "Why he is saying like that?". But I obeyed him without any idea. He always used to say about my marriage that it is a big part of my life. He opposes the concept of love marriage. Sure he said that his marriage is a arranged marriage.

Up to fifth standard, I have studied in co-education having no connection with the opposite gender. I have no ideas about them and their behavior. Till my higher education, I studied in women's college. We made a lot of discussions about marriage. But in specific, my life was empty. I have no idea about marriage. Everyone in my circumstances always speaks about my marriage and makes me afraid all the time. So, "Who will choose my life partner?" the question arose. "Me or my surroundings?" I asked in my mind. I studied in the government school but that area was surrounded by Muslims. So they are very strict in their culture. They are not allowed to mingle with the opposite gender. They were just shown the life partner; they need to marry without knowing them before. This is also a good culture even safe too.

Next, when I was going through my under graduation life, I got an opportunity to use social media. Through it, I got linked with the world and learnt a lot of things about marriage and life. Only with well - known members, I initiated my conversations. The reflection, I spoke with the opposite gender through it. Only my class members and relatives. Through making conversation, I got some improvement in understanding about "Why I need to marry?". Afterwards, I realized the truth that only through conversation, we can find the perfect one to marry. All my ways are accepted by my parents. They allowed me to use social media. But I handled it in a safe medium. All my movements are open to everyone. So everyone started to accept my ways and principles. The main fact was through all my journey God is with me. I used to read the Holy bible every day. Not only holy Bible, all the inspirational books I started reading to find the answer to the question "Why should I marry?"

Marriage is considered as a big part in every individual's life. For finding a life partner, there is a lot of ways. Through public places, online, working place, temples, church etc... But, I have only one option and that was to go through online. So, I handled it wisely. Then I started reading many articles about marriages. I got many ideas. However, I realized that marriage is the main part of my life. Because my parents come with me up to one limit. After that their support will vanish. So, this is the right time I need to marry. One woman cannot live alone without her life partner. In the same way, men also cannot survive without their partner.

All my circumstances deeply watching my life and concerning my life. So it makes me scared, even though I am accompanied with God's presence in me. Even for my small movements, everyone questions a lot. I need to answer them patiently. This is my situation. But I went along with my journey courageously to find answers for the unanswered questions about marriage. Everyone started criticizing my ways. But my movements are visible to everyone and they know I am in a safe border. My study centre, my home, my relatives, everyone knows about my life more than me.

But along with God's power, each answer I got about my marriage. He guided me either through holy books or other scriptures. My strict father supported all my ways. Because he started believing in me strongly more than me. He knows I don't speak with the opposite gender without any unwanted reasons. Now, he is not strict to me and also I understood why my father warned me in my childhood about the opposite genders. I understood that all my father's words has only saved me. And all his guidance is good for me. He gave me an option now to choose my life partner as my wish. He no more forces me for arranged marriage now. When I will find the perfect one, I will get married that day. God Bless All.

*****

"Marriage is a constant journey from untruth to truth about yourself and the world.
Since our world resides in our partner"

- Debashish Bindra

CAGED

By: Tritrishna Ghosh

I was considerably wistful whenever the topic of marriage crossed my path in these bygone years. From my childhood, I had a notion regarding this. It was a ceremony between two families while the boy and the girl tie the knot and make others happy. Everybody gets invited to participate in and life becomes a fairy tale ending.

But, over the years, this idea of marriage has changed its ambience around me.

Being the younger one of the two siblings, my parents never got bothered about my marriage until my elder sister does. It's a customary thing running around my family that the elder one needs to get married first. It's not that I am upset over this or whatsoever but these helped me ponder over the question of getting married a slightly better.

My parents got busy with choosing groom for my sister and I started witnessing the dilemma of close people being in marriage.

My fantasy of getting married turned into a nightmare overnight with the news of my paternal uncle's daughter getting beaten by her husband. When I went to see her, she still was not ready to blame her husband or leave him for her good. I was astonished by this commitment. What was preventing her from speaking, the fear of society or promise of safe shelter under a roof called home? Till date, I could not comprehend.

I told myself after this, all are not bad. Exceptions are the key to happiness. I am going to find the perfect one. Love will find its way overcoming all the obstacles and I too, will get decked up as a princess for my elegant journey to be a bride. But to my utter dismay, this saga continued.

My best friend eloped the following year with a boy to build a castle of their happiness which did not turn out so well for her. After nine days of marriage, she came to my house and told me about the torment she is undergoing in her husband's house. I could recall her words clearly, "Is this man I got married to? I could not relate. What has happened to our love?"

I was teary-eyed but no reply of mine could satisfy her. My senses were numb with the unsatisfactory life she chose for her and with the reflection that what if the marriage has something identical stored in for me. The deep dark bowl of unhappiness related to married life was encircling my sensibility.

The last nail in the coffin came when my elder brother got divorced and my sister-in-law filed a 498A against him. My brother who never killed a mosquito or yelled his voice out has beaten her wife was beyond imagination. It was a love marriage. They went out together for four years. I just simply couldn't understand when or where everything went wrong. But I tried hard to make things as they were before.

My brother was taken by the police as it was a non-bailable offence. We still wanted to sort things out. We talked with her and also her family. What she replied still makes me jittery. She mumbled, "Your brother didn't do anything. He has not beaten me. I just want alimony and divorce from him as I am in love with someone else. Your brother is an emotional fool. He won't leave me so I filed a case against him"

I was taken aback by her audacity. I was speechless too. My vision of marriage got ruined that very instant. How pathetic a human can become after they get married. As if the same person before and after marriage turn altogether, into a completely different entity. I was losing my mind and faith in the marriage too.

Though we had to fight a lot to get him out of her clutches, this situation taught me one thing, marriage is just not for me. Trust, love, promises cannot exist in my dictionary, after these encounters.

Being single and not ready to mingle became my life mantra to survive. My father once said, "Circumstances builds individual." I guess my life was meant to be different. I don't need to get married to live a happy and fulfilling life.

Some things are just not meant for some people and I am one of those people. Marriage does not belong to me and I don't belong to it.

*****

"Conveniences can never make for a successful marriage but for the mutual effort beyond self completes the bond"

- *Vidya Sampath*

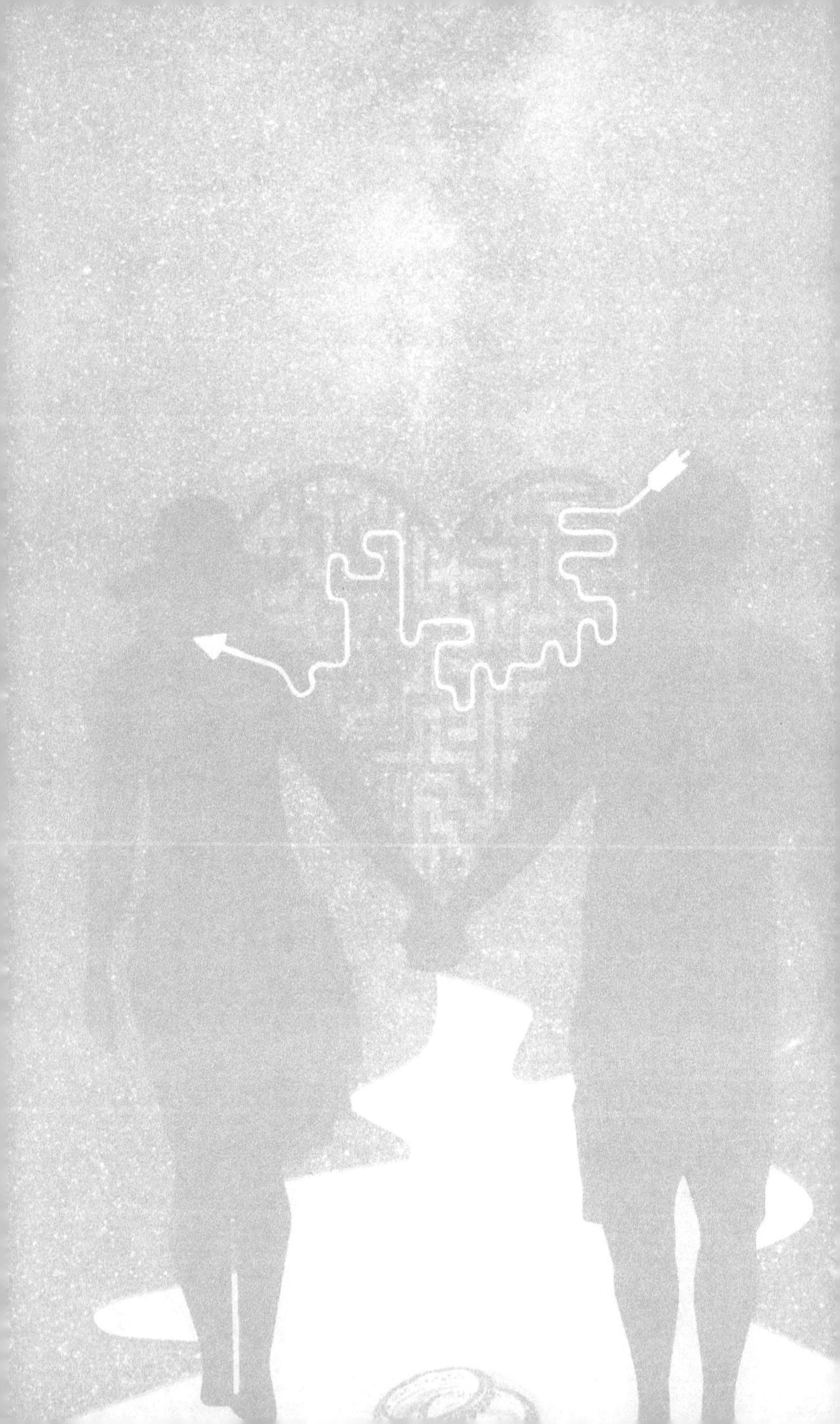

DESERVING

By: Lamiya Siraj

S tarting with my name – Ah! does it matter? If not, then let's go ahead with my views and opinions about marriage. With few incidents which happened during the different stages in life, my opinion kept changing. In my childhood, I saw the most troubled relationship in marriage between the couple whom I was closest to. Their thinking and decisions never matched with each other. They were the most suffered human-beings, staying together. *These couples made me decide that marriage is the last thing on earth I want to do!*

Moving ahead, till my teenage, I witnessed a few couples and their successful married life. The understanding and maturity between them were commendable. Respecting each other and handling the hardships of life, they opened my mind and made me think the other way around of giving marriage a chance.

But the question that kept hammering me was – Do I need a life partner? Why do I need a life partner? What is the need for having someone in my life, giving away all my freedom and sharing everything? Can I not lead my life alone? Am I not enough for myself? Such questions haunted me and kept me hooked up for a couple of years till I reached my adolescence. Soon I became an adult for my extended family and society. They started behaving as if I am a task, they need to complete by getting me married. I was overburdened every day with some or the other proposal. Getting irritated and just to dust off the responsibilities from my shoulder I accepted to meet few chosen ones.

Finally, one of the candidates who is my better half now, I never felt that strange bell ringing, when we met for the first time, as I had read in romantic novels or seen in movies. Either I didn't want to accept the reality or was in my fantasy world, not sure but yes, I was waiting for something like the music in the movie *'Mohhabbatein'* to happen with the falling of autumn leaves. Slowly and gradually I realized that practical life is far beyond the fantasies we create for ourselves.

I still remember how at the first instant I had rejected my life partner declaring he looks like a 'Lout'. But as said by wise and experienced people in the world, an opinion should not be formed in the first meeting or on looks. So, with maturity, I took time to understand him. I met him for a couple of times before giving away my biased opinion not being judgmental. Life, at the same time, has its plan and tragedies stored in for everyone. As soon as I decided to take one step ahead in my life by getting married to him, the real struggle started. We hardly knew each other and had taken our vows to be together forever.

With passing days, I realized how understanding, caring and loving he is! He not only understood me but stood by me strongly. He gave me the freedom to dream by adopting all my dreams as his responsibilities to fulfill. Then, be it a childish dream or a desire that was next to impossible, to be fulfilled. We both were coming from not so good backgrounds financially. Still, it's him who fulfilled my dream of travelling to various places in the world. My passion for knowledge and he made sure I complete my graduation and do my masters. Till date, when our daughter is in secondary school, I am still adding certificates to my folder.

I have the answers to my questions which I had some two decades ago, that 'WHY SHOULD I GET MARRY?' .We, as an individual, might be perfect but we as life-partners help each other to grow and flourish. Individually we may or may not achieve our dreams or desires but being together we cherish the accomplishments. Happiness is doubled. As a coin has two sides, the same goes with marriage! A Lot of sacrifices, honesty and patience are required. Sincerity and loyalty are the virtue of it. Trust is the pillar of marriage. It does have dark days when we are left shattered and broken. This is the time when we must support each other. At times, must let go of our ego and learn to adjust, adopting the change. Marriage is two souls getting ONE and families getting united. I have maintained a habit that we talk freely about our feelings, worries and fears. We believed in each other since starting.

So moral of my debate here is 'YES'. We don't need to fight our battles alone, we don't need to struggle alone, and the people who love us are our greatest source of strength. Always should keep them close and anything is possible, by God's will.

Today, being married for almost two decades now, I want to confess, my husband is the reason for everything GOOD in my life!

*****

"Marriage is the union of two different people having the same sense of belonging. It is all about finding the right person"

- Drishti Srivastava

HONEY TRAP

By: Harshika Seth

olaaaa!I am a girl full of ambitions, who carry her dreams in her eyes, who dreams of travelling the entire world with incredible experiences and enjoy the freedom but the truth is something else. Let me explain you, "She is looking young, now marry her off."

"This is the right time to seek a guy for her."

"Now let her go off (as if I am an old object to dispose of now)."

These are some of the statement what we hear regularly from childhood in our country. Did not found anyone asking what are our dreams, what we want to do, do we want to marry. By this time, you would have guessed my origin. Yes! I am from a typical stereotype country where girls are view as an object to just get marry and be a housewife. This is what I always saw since childhood. I saw how girls are forced to marry at a young age without their consent. Although we have laws against it so it took a new avatar of let get them engaged than after legal age they can marry. I always had a grudge against boys, they don't have to listen to this stereotype statements which hurt me like murdering something; probably my ambitions.

Woah... are you thinking I will be talking about the long old story of how girls are victimized in name of marriage? No. Although I was sad with the way my relatives and society looked upon me (getting married as soon as possible) I somehow managed to escape this trap and pursue my dreams.

While I was working with a multinational company, on one casual evening, while gossiping with the colleagues I came across something which leads me into deep thought.

My colleague was a handsome, muscular young guy of my age. "It does not matter of whom I like or love" he said.

"Why so?" I asked astonishingly.

"He is engaged since a very small age. And to whom he is engaged he does not know her well." another colleague said.

I was dumbstruck for a moment. I realized that my idea of forced marriage was bias to girls only. Not only girls but boys are forced too. My idea of hating boys because they were free to do what so ever fall apart.

But the question arises why? I have always seen relatives and friends forcing this guy is perfect for me that guy is perfect for me. Oooo hello! Am I not mature enough to choose my life partner? If not, then why am I marrying someone in the first place.

The idea of marriage solely depends on individual choices and perspective. No one should be forced; no one has the right to do this. I don't know if pairs are made in heaven but what I know that two soul and body need to have understanding, consent, love, and support to be together. This cannot be known by anyone other than the girl and boy marrying each other. A society cannot tell that they can be the perfect couple for life then why are they simply forcing. I feel marriage cannot be the sole aim of life, it's an intricate part of it which needs to embrace not forced.

A marriage which is a lovely experience imagined as a child but traumatic experience imagined by an adult.

Probably because we are forced to accept a partner which just because they fit the constraints laid by society as a whole.

I feel marriage is a most cherishable and rightful when we don't fell for a honey trap laid by society. We can always have happily-ever-after when we choose wisely with whom we want to spend our life's.

*****

"Love deep- rooted in a heart, a level higher valuing with marriage"

- Gayathri Ramasamy

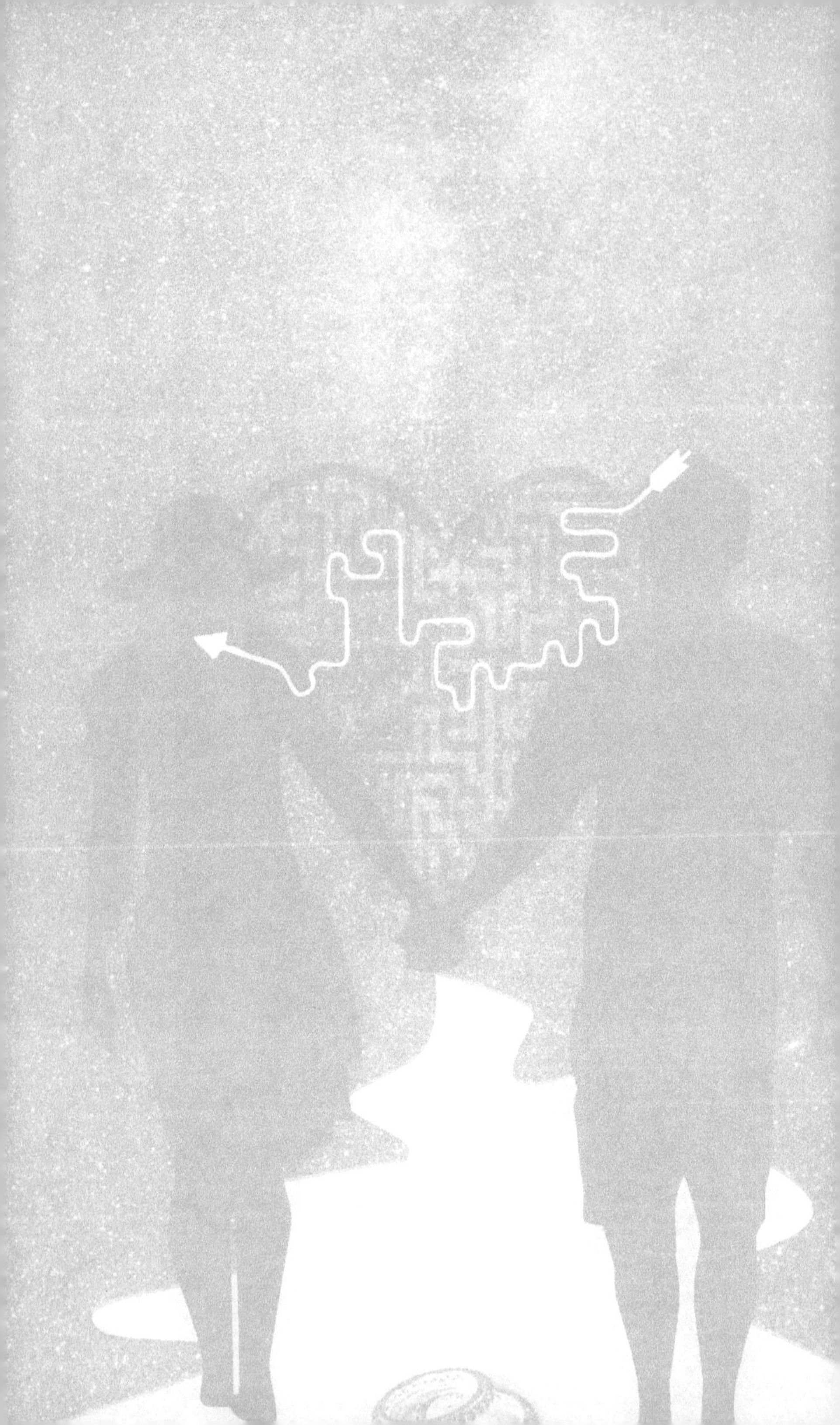

CHANGE OF WEATHER

By: Shyni Kayathri

Why should I marry? is the million-dollar question that arises amidst every young girl. Some wish to know the actual meaning; some don't care about it while the majority of them just go with the flow. At every stage of my life, I had different opinions about marriage. My opinion kept on changing like the weather. I was raised in a single-parent family and it was hard during the initial stage for both me as well as my mom. So that seed of scare against marriage was automatically sown.

As a teen, I grew up watching movies which made me misunderstand the concept of marriage, where the movie ended once the hero and heroine get married. Then I began to live in a fantasy world where I dreamt about a charming prince coming in a chariot to marry his princess and it enounced happy ending to me. But when days passed, I got to know that the second innings of life get starts only after the marriage.

However, one antithetical question too never fails to rise in me often, "Can anyone imagine life without getting married?" I have heard many of my friends telling me that they'll never marry until they are settled. It might work in the case of men but for women, it remains just a dream for the most part. The girl besties who spoke about a settlement have now tied a knot. And some others consider that marriages are made for fools. Yes, you read it right! This notion is especially familiar among 2k minds. Though the phrase looks modern it is impossible to live such in a society where the influence of kith and kin is at the peak.

Relatives play a major role in deciding my marriage age, time, place and even to whom, though I don't roll out a welcome mat for them. "When are you going to tie a knot?" is their never-ending interrogation which is quite annoying. Now I'm just 24 and I wonder, "Is any perfect age to get married?" And even if the weather changes and starts fluctuating towards getting married, these kindred obstruct my journey. Sticking to the wicked system of caste, they indirectly determine my marriage pattern. "Love marriage! Oh...no, it spoils our orthodoxy; Don't even think about it!", the trail of ceaseless advice sets off. They do reveal the tragic stories of marriage which make me bounce back often. At times, I feel I am an actor and my life is directed by someone.

No matter how the dilemma whirls the inner self; despite all odds and fears, everyone has their wedding dreams and I am not an exception. I prefer love marriage over an arranged marriage. Though it seems to be crazy, I believe in love at first sight, butterflies in the tummy and the unexpected proposals with a bunch of red roses. I have my dreams starting from the *sangeet* till the dinner at the reception. Though transitory, such moments are ever-cherishable. Having no constraints, my dream went beyond the fantasies of the wedding ceremony.

I once had a misconception that love is the only fuel that drives me to the desired destination but later on,

I realized it's not so. I opened my doors to reality and wish to lead a rational life. Now I have rebooted my mind to undertake a journey packed with love, care, respect and compatibility. Once I made a frame and sought my partner to perfectly fit in it. "Expecting a partner to be perfect in all aspects is a perfect example of an imperfect relationship", later I understood.

I need to live out the cute Tom and Jerry relationship which promises fun-filled, realistic romance. I want to be a holistic spiritual companion while excavating the treasures of *Loveland*. Finally, I'm ready to set sail for a voyage with a co-captain who facilitates the trip towards eternal bliss. I realized the change in my weather then I stopped predicting the passage of life, based on the stories heard and started to pen down my own. I wish that the magical essence of love in weather stays forever and offers a conducive climate for a successful journey of my marriage life.

*****

"If the love between two souls is destined for eternity, then marriage is the sacred journey to reach the infinity"

- Talima Das

TERMS AND CONDITIONS

By: Sagar Chavan

Aloha. I am just another Indian boy who grew up with their family, fortunate enough to get to learn basic things about the world and around through my elders.I am confident about saying yes or no to the Marriage stuff all because of the girls I met with terms and conditions. This always gave me negative feelings about marriage. Our elders always taught us that marriage is a lifetime bond where you just accept each other unconditionally. These always made me think I'm going to have someone in my life that will understand & accept me the way I am. I would do anything for that one girl. Let's call her my Harley Quinne.

From childhood, I was very fond of beauties and cuties hope you get me what I mean by these two terms. So I was giving my 100% whenever I get a chance to impress a girl in any way possible & that's what I did from childhood to date. I completed college and currently working. In this span of time, I got proposed by many girls to be honest. I believe in a relationship with **NO STRINGS** attached & just have fun. Then a time came in my life where I understood that now it's time to be serious. I need to find a girl to marry and I need to stick to a girl for a lifetime. As I already said I am working in a Company and there I met a beautiful girl. In a very short span of time, we were more than friends. We used to spend a lot of time talking on calls and that's how it started. Finally, I asked her what kind of guy you want as a husband. She said he must have a huge salary (double than her), he should have his flat in this City on his name it doesn't include the home where he stays with his mom and dad, he should give me my personal space and he should not interfere in my personal life. He should not be like adjust with this adjust with that & so on her list started made me think I am lucky I'm not getting married to her.

Then I thought of going to arrange marriage. My parents selected a girl. We visited their home and all would go good until I ask so what your wish or conditions for getting married and every single girl would answer with a smile not much just a few things they are:

1.   Own Home (not on rent)

2.   Good Salary (Satisfy need of both in monetary ways)

3.   To stay alone after marriage not with Mom & Dad (so no Mother-in-law problem)

This thing was told to me in different ways from different girls, I know that it's not something wrong to ask from your future partner as she has to spend the rest of the life with me so she just wants to be secured mentally and financially. Yes,I accepted their thoughts and in all these conditions I was lucky enough as I was satisfying the top two conditions with god's grace. But that 3RD Condition made me a bit annoyed. I can't leave my parents for anyone else. Some people may think staying away is always better but I think if in old age, you can't be with your parents you are of no use for them. Because they will never ask for money from you they would only ask for the time to spend with you. My parents readily agreed to all the conditions as they wanted me to settle. I decided to marry a girl who is ready to accept my family, or else l was better alone. That is the reason I'm still single. Sometimes I think I should get back to the old me and enjoy life the way I use to but on the other hand, somewhere down the line I know it's wrong to do so. Because it's awesome in a sense to stay in many rental homes and enjoy the new place every time. But then you miss that own home feel where you feel safe and feel no one else can ask you to leave as it's our own home & just as this example I wanted a partner for forever not just for a short span of time. I want to have that one person with me for the rest of my life with whom I can grow old together with my family. It's my only condition to get married to any girl and I don't know why I'm not so lucky to find that right girl that's why I decided not to marry till I find the right one. But, I live a happy life both financially and mentally too. As I'm happy I don't change my mind and I am taking care of my parents. I just don't pay their expenses also I spend time with them. Hence I always answer my mom when she says you should get married as your age is growing and I always say the same if I marry. I will marry and stay together with you all or better I stay single.

If I need to accept their terms tend condition and get married and stay away from my parents, Where I'll not be happy in the real term so tell me why should I marry..?

*****

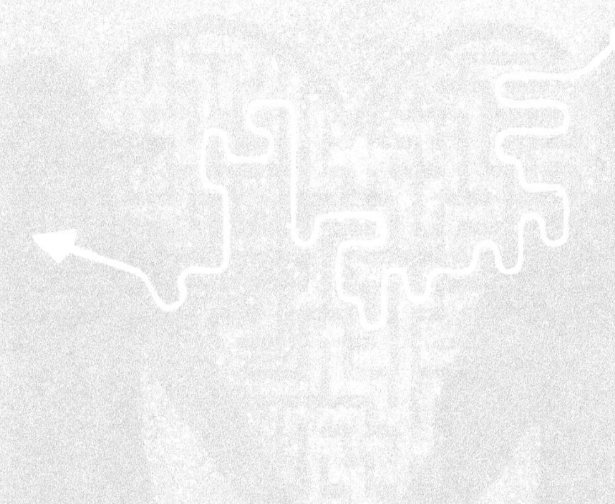

Marriage is not just a union of two people or families instead it's something beyond anyone's imagination.

- Panchanand Gupta

CONSTRUCTIVE IMAGINATION

By: Aviral Tripathi

J ust like some people are gifted with the powers to be leader, to be able to understand people's intentions, I was lucky enough to get the power of imagination. I am an engineering student cum writer. These imaginative powers often take me into situations that I have never actually been in.

I was travelling back to my hometown, after nearly two years of constant efforts for not going back there, for my friend's wedding. I had always avoided going back there. Even in my college holidays, I used to make absurd excuses to my parents for not coming back. The reason for this is the nostalgia of my love story it holds, from which I am continuously escaping. The nostalgia had started its effect and the memories of that beautiful night of winter walking hand-in-hand with her flashed in front of my eyes. I barely avoided an accident. I went directly to Gaurav's home, instead of mine.

"You came Avi, you came. I am so happy to see you, brother," said my friend Gaurav with that carefree look he always had. I congratulated him and smiled back. Anmol was already there.

These two people were the gems of my school life.

While chit-chatting with them, Gaurav asked both of us about our plan for marriage. I just escaped the question, although my parents too had been asking me to get married.

But Anmol answered it with a question, "Why should I marry?"

The conversation, although, went on to several other topics, but I was stuck at that one question.

Later on the day, I went to my house. While lying on the bed, I was lost in my imaginations.

I was sitting on a sofa dressed in a *Sherwani*, with an unknown girl standing beside me. There was hustle and bustle everywhere, with hundreds of people all around.

I was being engaged, with a 'so-called best girl for me' about whom I know nothing because my family chose her.

The Engagement was completed successfully and they had planned my marriage in the next 2 months.

The plans and preparations started as soon as the Engagement was over. All my cousins were over my head, trying to pull my legs at each opportunity they had. But, where I was to enjoy their teasing or to get irritated at them. I was completely occupied with the pre-wedding jitters.

I may have been nervous, and terrified with the idea of marriage, but moreover, I was anxious about one damn question i.e. Why should I marry?

While I was busy exploring my question, I got a call from my fiancée which further added to my frustration. She wanted to meet me before the wedding and expressed her desire to know me. I agreed, as she was at least sensible enough to understand how important it is to know each other, although I had the least interest in knowing her.

Without letting anyone know, we met at a temple outside the main town. Always being the worst at starting a conversation, I didn't even try to break the awkward silence. Finally, she broke the silence, and her first few words left me dumbstruck. She asked me the reason for not being interested in the marriage. It was as if she has spellbound me through her words, that I uttered all my insecurities and anxiety in front of her, from my love story to the question in my mind.

She listened to every single word patiently, and when I was over with it, she told me about hers.

Her company felt extremely soothing, something I have been wandering for years. We sat under a tree with a magnificent view in front of our eyes. It was again she who broke the silence, this time a tranquillizing one.

She said, "We never usually move-on from our first love. We just increase our capacity to give love, hence enabling ourselves to love two persons at a time." She added, "Loving more than one person at a time doesn't make you wrong. And if it does, then how come loving your wife is right when you already love your mother?"

These words made a much deeper impact than anyone can imagine. They made me capable of doing something I have been restricting myself from, i.e. loving. She caught me looking at her smile and blushed.

This romantic moment faded away as I was dragged out of my imaginary world by my caller tune. Gaurav had called to ask me to come over to his house. I got up from my bed, changed the clothes, and left the home.

Those were not her memories that bound me, it was me who restricted myself and her memories. Now, I had restored my freedom, and so did her memories.

My imaginary marriage taught me the most important lesson of my life.

*****

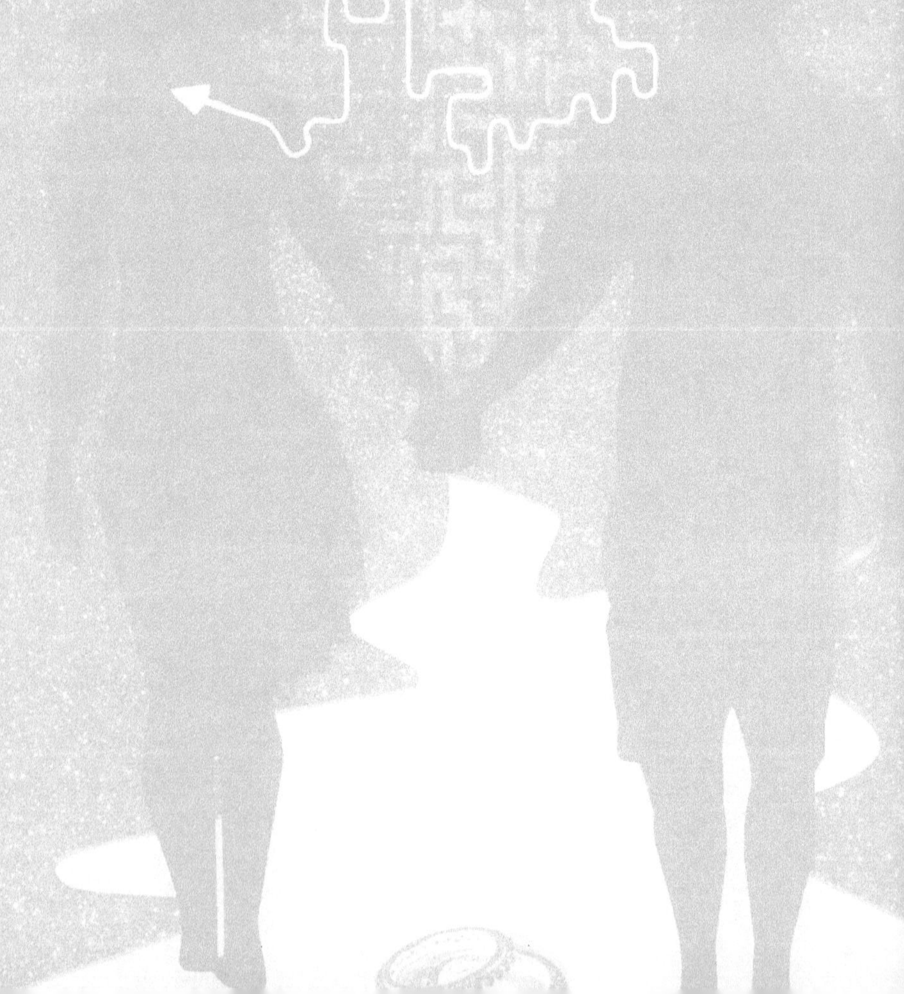

"When its love there's no need to arrange it, marriage is just a name of binding two souls together sometimes with permission, sometimes without attention"

- Vinay J

RAINBOW OF LOVE

By: Dr. Anmol Pandey

Marriage is a very confusing concept in our country. We have many types of wedding; arranged, love arranged, love marriage etc.

Even after all this, I loved this concept of marriage in my childhood days.

Those beautiful dresses, tasty foods, shopping, everyone treats you like a princess; these materialistic things kept me fantasizing for a long time. But when I step out from dream world to the real world these things started to look a bit fuzzy.

I have seen so many successful weddings and many broken ones also. So, when I saw the world with my own experience then I realized that wedding doesn't just bring happiness, it brings many responsibilities, adjustments and sometimes situations where we have to think about someone else and not just about ourselves.

Now, "when will you get married?"isthe most common question the age group of 20 -25 would come across as if marriage is a competition in which one should take part and should win also.

Okay, jokes apart, I guess marriage is a relationship which can last only if both of them are physically, emotionally and mentally connected. One thing which I never understood is why people are waiting for the soul mate

I mean, is there someone who will come and say, "Yes, I am your soul mate. Let's get married." ?? I don't think so.

The concept of soul mate is so hyped in our generation that people forget the reality that no relationship is formed by itself. It develops gradually, so the day you will realize that a person you are living with is your soul mate, you may already bein your fifties!!

So, as I told in the beginning, we have many types of a marriage; arranged, love, love arrange etc . It can be successful only if two people want it to be.

A stranger can be your soulmate and maybe the person you are thinking about is not!

Surprised!!!

People say get married when you are ready, but who will tell that you are ready or not??

Because most of the time our decisions are just a result of the things that are happening around us, if someone has a boyfriend or girlfriend then they really wanna get married soon. If someone had a recent break up, he/she probably never wanna get married.

So I think there is no perfect answer to the question 'when should I get married'. Like other Indian girls, I also dreamed of a perfect fairy tale marriage, a successful marriage.

But I'm not going to wait for someone to come and tell me that yes I am your soul mate.

I want to get married when I'm ready for a change when I'm ready to adjust, ready to compromise with my comfort zone.

I want to get married when I am ready to give everything for that one relation and with the person who is also ready to do so.

Because that's what relationships are all about.

No matter if that person looks like my soul mate and my dream boy or not!!

But till then it's not a bad idea to explore in life, to see all aspects so that one could be mature enough to handle the ups and downs.

Till then I'm just going to paint my imaginary canvas with all my favorite colors and when I will finally find someone. We will mix our colors make our life a beautiful rainbow, full of color which includes both, the sunlight and a thunderstorm.

*****

"Marriage is not only just a word, it is a strong bond of true and lucid relations of two pure souls which always in too deep"

- **Jayashree Sahoo**

HAPPILY EVER AFTER

By: Shamim Merchant

arriages are settled in heaven but celebrated on Earth. The unity of two unknown souls written right from birth." This was imprinted on my wedding card twenty eight years ago, when I was 22. Little did I know the value and importance of marriage at that tender age.

I was born and brought up in a huge joint family, four uncles and their increasing kinship. While growing up, I witnessed both long happy married lives and heartbroken relationships. And every aspect that I testified, was a learning experience for me and my future.

A joint family means responsibilities and compromises. At least this is what we saw our parents doing. Trying to keep everyone happy and in the process of doing so, they had to bow and bend innumerable times. In spite of that, they always served others whole-heartedly and that too with a smile. I guess that also has a satisfaction of its own.

When I stepped into my new home with my husband, I had entered with a lot of apprehensions and anticipations. Is he the man of my dreams? Will it work? Although we both come from the same cultural and religious background, we are two different individuals with unique personalities and specific beliefs and ideas. But love, respect, patience and the perseverance to succeed, kept us going. Definitely, life hasn't been a bed of roses. We've had our ups and downs and our differences too.

Nevertheless, today, after having celebrated my silver anniversary and a proud mother of two young and dashing boys, I can complacently tell that yes, everyone must get married. It may have its disadvantages, but those are just a few. There are plenty of pros. Let me tell you how beautiful marital life can be.

It's extremely important to be realistic. Bollywood types, filmy love stories are good to fantasize about, but reality can be shocking if you don't face it practically. I always knew that my husband is not a prince charming in shining armour, nonetheless he is a good, simple and an honest man with zero addiction of any kind. Isn't that a great quality?

Marriage gives you that love and happiness which you've been seeking all your life. You become important and special for someone. There is always someone to talk to, who would listen to you and cry with you in your pain. We come from a middle class family and lead a simple life. In 28 years, we have faced many challenges, but vital is that neither of us was ever alone. We were always there for each other.

Married people knows that there's someone waiting for you to come back home. It gives you a sense of comfort and security. Not just the concrete walls and roof on top, but a surrounding filled with warmth and love. My husband has never allowed me to stay more than ten days at my mom's place. He would always say, "Shama, come back soon. I don't like it without you."

Depression has no place in a couple's life. Invariably there is your better half either to make you feel better or to become your temporary punching bag. Children grow up in a safe and respectful environment. They learn from their parents the value of relationships and what it means to keep peace and stay tied to someone for a longer haul.

Of course every person is going to talk about his or her marriage as per their experience. An unhappy man will have a different story to tell. Like the great personality Socrates had said, "By all means, marry. If you get a good wife, you'll become happy; if you get a bad one, you'll become a philosopher."

It isn't just essential to find the right life partner, it's more important to become the right one for your spouse too. If you become his dream girl, then surely he will also transform to be the man of your dreams.

I have found my happily ever after, I hope you find yours too.

*****

"Marriage is a book written in the language of love, using the syntax of trust and dialect of care by two tender hearts"

- Anita Shinde

CONNECTION

By: Mohammed A.

Why should I marry you? We have loved each other but was it the only reason to marry you? You're neither rich nor talented...do you really deserve to marry me?" All these words ramble in Ashok's mind with the same freshness even after three years.

Ashok's love life with Abinaya began while pursuing his MBA degree. Ashok is now chasing his life between dream and reality. Though he has successfully completed his degree, he is facing a difficult time in finding a job and setting up his career. He had approached almost 30 companies for employment but still couldn't even get one. He also gets few temporary opportunities and he will work hard to prove him and make it permanent but his misfortunes continues and he has pushed to search for another job. Though pains and burns are there, he is never depressed over this external pain. Because he was never looking for a richer life but a happy life with his soul mate Abinaya. When our heart is filled with love, external pain cannot penetrate and weaken us.

But life has twists and turns in its own way. His dream started to collapse slowly day by day from the past six months. The love and care was not happening. Because the life of Abinaya was quiet the opposite of what he is facing now? She got an almost clear path and was busy with her new circle. Whenever Ashok tries to reach her, she is always occupied with her schedule and her new network of friends. She is not there either to give or to receive love and care.

He realized that his love is going to end slowly but unfortunately, he is just a mute spectator now. He has taken the option of creating beautiful memories until it exists. So, he put his maximum efforts even if it is for few minutes in a day. And all the time they met, he made something to see her smiling and fill those memories deep in his heart. Days of six months ran fast like days of a week. One fine day she bid goodbye to him. Although he knew that it would happen, he was not prepared for the last day. His world froze there when she gave the reason and told him that she didn't want to be in that relationship anymore. Except telling 'ok, as you wish, he can't add or give any justification. A 5 year love finishes its journey in a 5 minutes call over phone. She had a completely different life now and Ashok can't be there by any chance. Also, Ashok never disturbed her after she told her decision to leave him.

Although Ashok is comfortable with his career life now, he is not happy. He feels emptiness in life and was not able to start that love and connection again. He recently experienced a few proposals which he felt initially ok to proceed but something happened inside him and he was not able to proceed further to dream of a love life again. Now everyone talks about Ashok's marriage. Some gave weird reasons for having marriage. He can't explain everything to everyone. So many times he keeps silence and sometimes he replies with phony reason.

When his uncle Ramu asked about his marriage plan, he sighed as he is going to answer to it for the

Eleventh time of the day. This time he just replied, 'I need to settle a little more in my career and will initiate the marriage process shortly. If you come across any matching alliance, please let me know'. And by the way, his uncle has already tired of bringing new alliances and he is rejecting them every time with new reasons.

In that late evening, tasting a cup of coffee and relaxing on a sofa he asked himself to find the real reason 'why I am not married yet?'. He closed his eyes and just recorded his thought in his diary as ' Is marriage all about forming a family and fulfilling sexual desires? If so, just for that marriage is not required. Then just the name 'marriage' will be distinguishing life of human and animal. Is it a contract to love and live with a person lifelong? Then why people are breaking it with the name of divorce and second marriage'. He paused his pen for a while and continued writing. 'Marriage is recognition for uniting two souls, they feel love for each other, they should mutually respect each other, they should exchange their thoughts, care for each other, feelings and views without any barrier and hesitation. And of course fulfilling sexual desires which is a part of it but not necessary it only gives the complete meaning. Because life in the 30's and life in the 60's are very different. When we are 60, we don't look for fulfilling the external desires but a strong connected relationship is the one we look for.

So accept the marriage proposal only if you feel that connection in your heart. There are some few cases where people who were in love were getting divorced after a few years of marriage and the reason is simply they have given importance for external things such as appearance, money and etc. and forget to feel the connection by heart. You can feel that connection either before marriage or after marriage but to do that one should be ready to love, respect and care for your counterpart'. He closed his diary and went for sleep.

Now Ashok is clear that why he shouldn't marry without love, respect and care. He is waiting to feel that connection again even though it takes some time.

*****

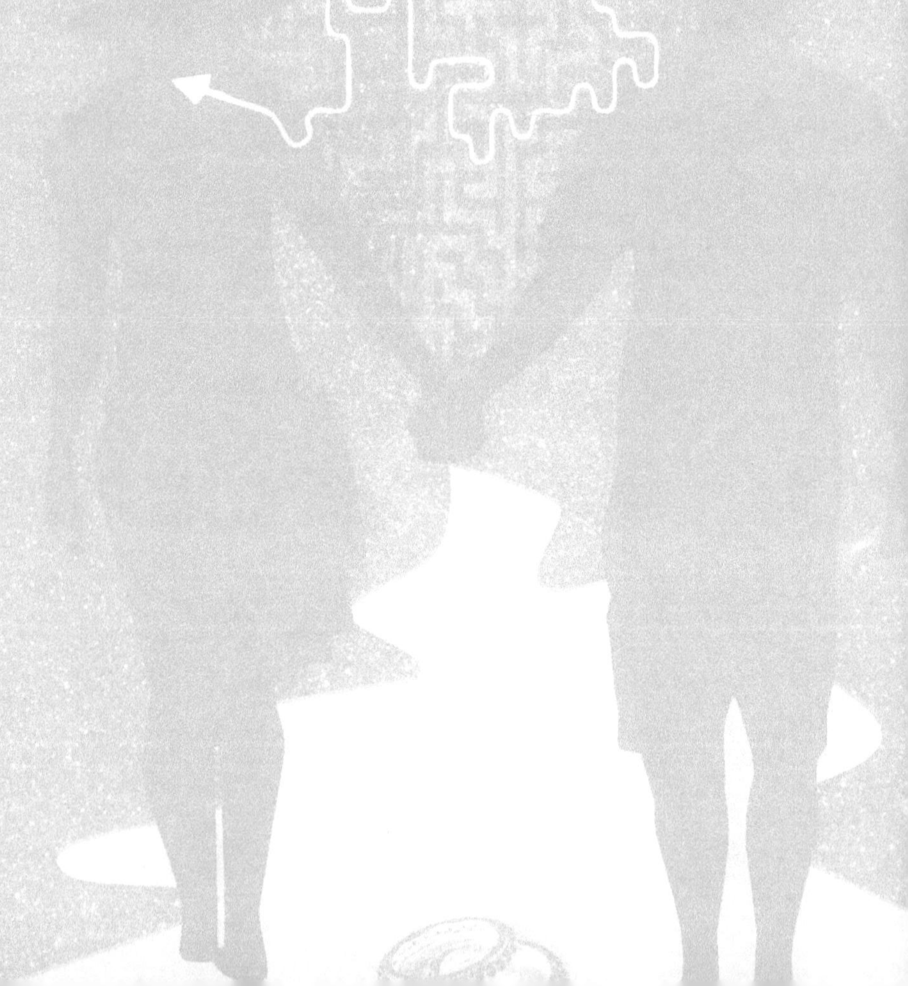

"Marriage is not a mere agreement to share only love and bliss, it's an invitation to accept and respect one another's idiosyncrasy"

- Danish P. R

WOUNDS OF HEART

By: Noor Tabassum

Sitting in the balcony, sipping a cup of tea, I kept wondering why does this world call me a rebel? Expressing one's thoughts freely is a freedom to be respected rather than rejected and insulted. The bitterness filled in me is not inborn. It has developed with time and worsening circumstances.

When I crawl through the memory lanes, what I have experienced justifies my behavior. I hate to visit my memory lanes, but I can't help myself from going through it. They don't leave me alone. They keep haunting and troubling me.

Being the only child of my parents, I was proud to be their prime attention. When I was very young, things were very happy and normal. Mom would usually narrate the stories of Snow White and Cinderella at bedtime to put me to sleep. A very beautiful and unique concept captivated my little mind. I always fantasized a handsome prince taking me to his fairyland with love and respect. It made me very happy. I would sleep dreaming of it.

I asked mom how she met dad? Mom blushed. She said that they had met each other in university. She took pride in saying that dad fell for her as soon as he saw her. He then started persuading mom. He would impress her in every possible way. Bouquets were given, songs were sung, and immense efforts were made to impress her. Love bloomed in both the hearts. Roses were red and sky was pink for both. Love had a Midas touch. It made everything wonderful.

Lovers become rebels if opposed. So was my parent's situation. They were not granted permission to marry as they belonged to different sects. But who cares when in love? They didn't bother to listen to their parents. Both were threatened to be thrown as outcast. They willingly agreed and without paying heed to anyone, got married.

Within a year, I was born to them as their symbol of love. Mom took great pride in telling this story to me. Initially, things were all magical. They would argue, but I was kept away from it. Both used to come out wearing plastic smiles which my innocent mind thought was true. But how long could they hide? Slowly their voices barged out of their bedroom door filling my heart with terror. I would panic. Things went on becoming so worse that the abusive music played every night at our home. It became my lullaby now. I wondered where did their love vanish. How did it fade so badly? Why are they together in the first place? Probably because of a fragile string and that's me. But in marriage, that string should be love and trust, otherwise it's not worth it.

Filled with excessive toxin in my mind and heart, I joined an NGO who work for women's upliftment. To my surprise, I saw most of the cases were of tortured women in marriage. They were beaten black and blue by their tyrant husbands. All these events have made me pessimistic towards this marriage concept.

I fail to understand why we marry. Is it because of society pressure? If so, why doesn't society protect us against these unbearable burdens. Is love guaranteed till death? And when love vanishes are we supposed to behave like brutes insulting each other and at times thrashing each other. I, then, understood why Romeo and Juliet never married and died before marriage. If they would have married, they would have also ruined their lives. It's my vision of seeing things. Marriages are meant to tie us together with respect and love. It should uplift us and not degrade us. When such questions haunt me, the world becomes judgmental and I am called a rebellion.

Today when I sit sipping my tea, I am happy to be free and safe. Safe from the clutches of emotional blackmails, mental torture, sentimental drains and depressions. I know that the poison in me is too bitter and deep rooted. Not all the marriages are disaster. Many have successfully lived it setting examples. But I am influenced by my bad experiences. I refuse to forget it.

I believe that I will need a partner who would be my best friend in the long journey of life. I am ready to wait till I meet that person who will recognize my pain and wait till my wounds are healed. Wounds of the heart are usually very slow to heal. I want a person who would restore the faith I have lost in marriage. Who will transform the hatred in my heart to abundant love? Till then, I am ready to be a single ghost. I refuse to give in to this whirlpool called marriage. I will never compromise with my self-respect.

*****

"*Marriage cannot sustain on leftover attention, it has to be continuous sustainable effort over a lifetime*"

- Rakhshinda Faizi Kidwai

JOURNEY

By: Archita Alipuria

Writing is not magical; it is a blessing that creates magic. This is what I woke up to, it's been more than a couple of years, I have been working on a novel and suddenly my train of ideas came to a dead end. Being a writer, when your mind is under the same roof for a long period of time, a bike ride to the nearest café library is essential for your artistic child. When I opened the door to the café I was welcomed with dulcet thunders of laughter and clouds of happiness. The aroma of coffee instantly calmed my stress for writing and made me lose myself in the world of imagination. Usually I would have picked up a self-help book or some murder mystery but that day my eyes fell on a love story. I have always believed in consuming content that you would have never consumed on a usual day to defeat your writer's block, because it opens your brain in certain ways. So here I was, eyes fixed on words and fingers wrapped around a warm heavenly mug.

Hours passed by and as always I kept no track of time. Reading rewires my brain; it's like escaping from the real world, forgetting about me and living the life of the character. Soon the book came to an end and the last chapter left me with tears in my eyes.

The story was about the main character getting married and facing some obstacles in her love life. This is the beauty of love, we all at some point of our life have been heartbroken or have been in love, I guess that is why it is always relatable. But I never had enough time or wanted to allow the thought of marriage wander in my mind but today the story left me with an impact, something magical that made me fall in the pond of thoughts.

Coming to my life, I have always found myself running on the highway leading towards success. I did have a past few relationships but the word marriage has always been synonymous to restrictions for me. I don't know why I believe behind the glamorous veil of Indian weddings lies a face full of tears. I have seen most of my friends giving up their successful careers for the sake of being settled. I have been career focused since my childhood, I always wanted to be a great writer. We just get one life to live and why waste that in standing up for societal expectations. Watching reality in the mirror, it won't be wrong to say marriages do change a person as an individual.

On the other hand, sinking deep, a part of me does believe in true love and would want to spend my life with someone who not only loves me but understands me. The one who is aware of all my flaws and hides them under his curtains so that the world could not see them, and I have seen all his tears and always made sure that I take all his pain in, no matter how much destruction is caused to me. I want to be in a relationship whose wheels are respect, not only self-respect but also respect for our opinions, values and morals. Where he would go to any extent to bring me close to my dreams and I will not fear for a second to do the same. Where we give each other all our feathers and weave wings the whole night, only to fly with the early morning with the sunrise. Once you find someone who prioritizes your smile over anything and makes sure that no one takes away your personal space, marrying them would be nothing but the start of a beautiful story. Many have argued that love changes after marriage, but I believe it all depends upon how much effort you are willing to put in. Most of the people end up being married before even knowing themselves, our entertainment industry has made us believe in a layered illusion of love that is why people fear marriage. Though it is a huge decision of your life, if taken wisely it can positively change your world.

I was journaling whatever came to my mind and was woken to reality by the café manager as they were about to close. I felt relieved and ideas started hitting my brain. Maybe I knew what I lacked in my novel now.

*****

"Whether law-driven or love-driven, let the souls decide which hand they want to hold"

- **Alpesh Chandora**

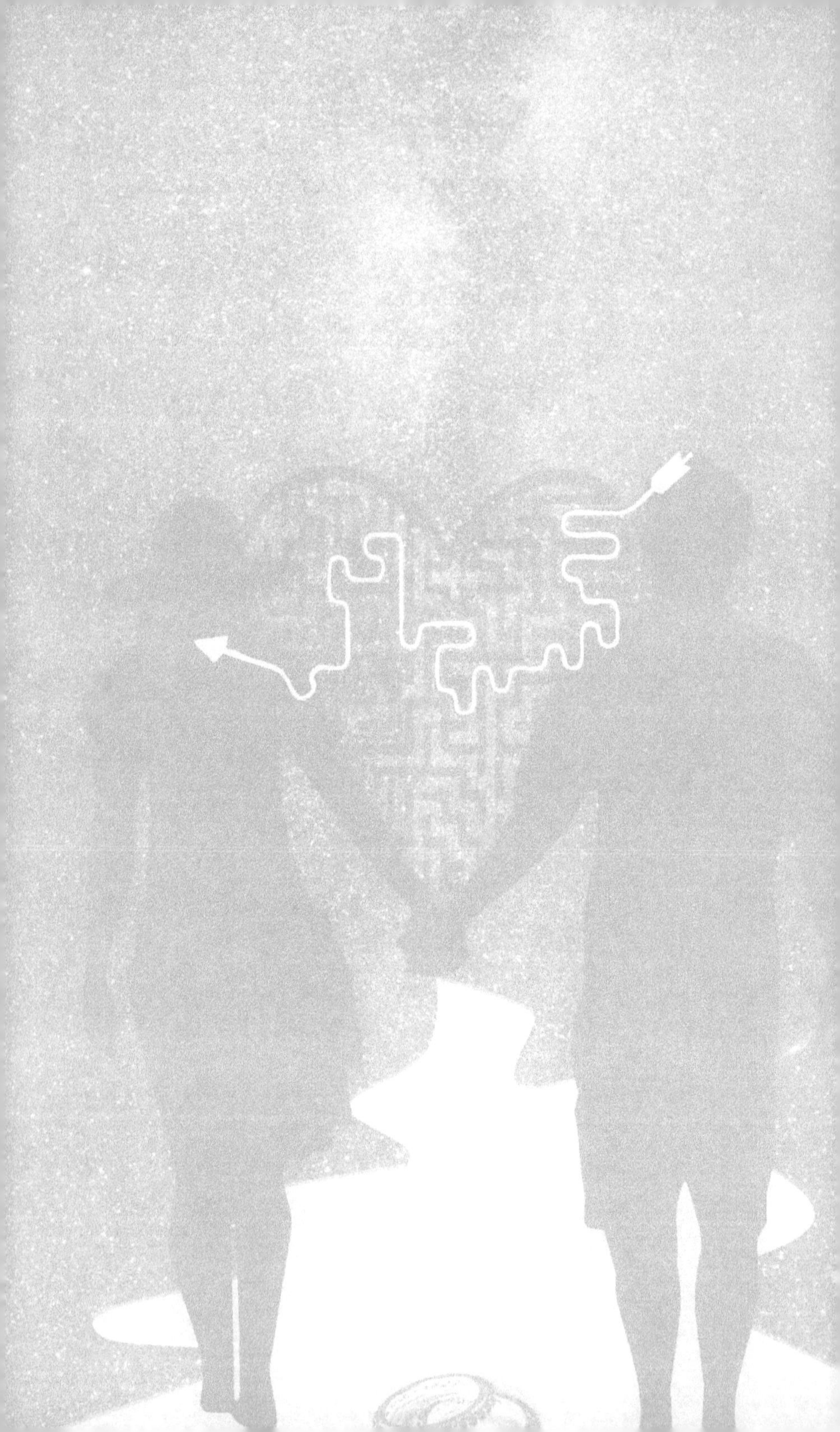

HARDLY A YES!

By: Kayathri Kumar

Kiara is my name, the bright soul wandering and wondering on Earth. My friends used to tease me by saying that I'm that weird alien accidentally pulled into Earth's gravity. Yep, I'm not any ordinary girl who's confined to rules but someone who wonders and seeks answers about purpose, existence and reason behind every ritual and phenomenon I encounter. Just because I question a lot, people find me weird. No, this is not some random weird story you would be reading sitting in your cozy sofa with the smell of coffee brewing from the cup kept nearby. This story is all, yet to conquer question of mine. It might be one of your unconquered quests too.

I turned 25 last week and I'm not married so far. If any orthodox parent would be reading this, they would definitely find me weird, "Instead of cooking dishes, what is she trying to cook in these pages?" Jokes apart, the thing is I haven't given much serious thought about marriage yet. But in recent days, this question about marriage somehow found its way into my neurons and has turned out to be the only question that constantly resides in me and keeps popping up often.

Turning back the pages of my life, as a kid, the term 'marriage' carried the fragrance of happiness. Yep, I can skip school for a day or two, wear a pretty dress, more importantly, eat as many chocolates as I can and play with lots of kids I haven't even met before. In a nutshell, it's a kind of occasion I can enjoy to the fullest.

Since I wasn't the protagonist of the event, it was a happy occasion for me. As an onlooker, that's what marriage meant in my little happy universe.

Eventually, as a teenager, the marriage took the synonym of Treasure Island, the journey being filled with excitement, thrill and surprises. I was neither aware of the journey nor the destination, but that didn't stop me from fantasizing about a perfect wedding with the anonymous prince charming. Those were the days the term marriage tagged a big bright blushing smile on my face. I even remember listing out the qualities my companion should have, not a big list though because all I cared about was 'Care.' The least you're aware of the destination, the more curious you would be they say; that was the case for me as a teenager who thought of marriage as a blissful destination. Maybe the essence of bliss vanquished the hardships marriages hold.

But once the comfort zones vanished, the reality started to smirk weirdly. My thoughts about marriage, being a happily ever after fairytale disappeared and reality gave a smack at my face bringing me to my senses. The moment I began to understand 'How marital institution works?'I started to question them, everything took a new different meaning in my dictionary, and the word marriage somehow failed to exist in it. The once thought fairy tale occasion turned into a scary tale in the meantime.

Sharing most of my life with girls right from schooling to college; I didn't get much chance to converse with boys and that made me even timid around boys. It was during my postgraduate course I got to converse with boys in my class. So, being less aware of the boys' community became another reason that I don't want to marry. Leaving my parents to live with the person neither I knew nor I have met or conversed before. It sounds not that good right?

'Love!' they say, but I've seen girls losing themselves in the journey and leading a tiresome life just for the sake of the sacred thread around their neck. Understanding is an important element in love, but understanding doesn't guarantee love. Only with understanding and respect for each other marriage becomes a successful journey they say, but who follows it? In the long run, one takes another for granted and the whole journey starts to stink, and it just functions based on compromises. No, I don't want to do that and be one of those victims. I feel like the delight, the excitement, the thrill and the surprises about marriage seems like a mirage. Once you get close to feel it, it's just not there. Marriage sounds like a scary nightmare adorned and narrated with beautiful and blissful lies that I once enjoyed, but not anymore.

Life is not a scientific problem where the trial and error method to answer life will help you disclose the answer; And not every question has an absolute answer, there are only better answers and the answers change with time. So, until I'm mentally prepared to take a big step in my life let me have my wardrobe filled with my favorites.

*****

"Marriage means the words 'yours' and 'mine' are rebuilt with the word 'ours'."

- Arshiya Patel

OUR SPONSORS

PRO RICH

Instagram Handle:
@manishbhatia69

Address:
Mumbai,Maharashtra

Pro Rich is a firm managed by Manish Bhatia-Mutual Fund Distributor and Insurance Agent.

Want to grow your money but not sure HOW and WHERE to invest?

You can Visit this link too,

Facebook:
https://www.facebook.com/manishbhatiainvestment/

Contact:

Cell: +919820191569

Email id: mbhatialoans@gmail.com

B.S.R A.S.A Diary 786

Yourquote Handle:
@bsr_asa_diary_786

Started on :
30th July, 2018

B.S.R A.S.A Diary 786 is a page on YourQuote app which takes you towards the Beautiful journey of Writing, where you can read heart touching poetries, shayaris, quotes and other forms of writings. This page is all about the experience of life and true feelings. Common language has been used in all the writings, so that the readers can be made aware of the purpose of writing. One can feel some hidden feelings and emotions by visiting this page.

Do check and follow this page for amazing experience.

Instagram : @b.s.r_a.s.a_diary_786

Visit the page via this link:

https://www.yourquote.in/bsr_asa_diary_786

Email Id : sadafrehan356@gmail.com

FRAME INN

FRAME INN

Instagram Handle:
@frameinn.in

Address:
Surat,Gujarat

Frame Inn is a digital media agency where we ideate and execute creative concepts for our clients to make them stand out from their rivals. We know how to blend technology and creative ideas which match our clients purpose and make their brand matter.

At Frame Inn, we work, unite and communicate as a family. Teamwork and Creativity is our top priority. Our creative team offers enthusiasm towards their job and dedication towards every particular project.

For more details, contact,

Email id : hello@frameinn.in

Website: www.frameinn.in

JK PARKER MIXER GRINDER

Instagram Handle:
@jkparker

Address:
Mumbai,Maharashtra

JK Parker Mixer Grinder is India's toughest mixer grinder. For making your kitchen work easy and grind tough objects with ease you should definitely buy JK Parker mixer grinders. To give best quality mixer grinder is the main motto of our company.

You can be a part of our family too. For buying our mixer grinder please do visit our website.

Website:

www.jkparker.in

TAQDEES ASSORTMENTS

Taqdees Assortments

Instagram Handle:
@taqdeesassortments

Address:
Honnavar,Karnataka

Taqdees Assortment is an online Assortment for women clothing as well as kids wardrobe. Unique kinds of Kurtis, palazzo sets, Pakistani suits, dress materials, Saree, chudidar, jumpsuits, kids clothes are available in our Assortments which will reinforce your elegance as well as kid's charm. Shipping is all over India. If you love wearing amazing garments then surely be a part of this Assortments.

Join us through what's up the group and stay tuned.

Contact:

Cell 1: 8296563570

Cell 2: 9591439044

A & M Fashions

Address:
Kanpur,Uttar Pradesh

Started On:
October, 2014

A & M Fashions Online Boutique offers a wide range of apparels, Hand Crafted Items & Fashion Accessories to fit any woman's unique sense of style. Our clothing and accessories are carefully curated to provide our customers the latest fashion. Our top priorities are excellent customer service, exceptionally quick order processing & ultra fast shipping times all across the globe.

Join through the following:

WhatsApp group Link

https://chat.whatsapp.com/DWWHTlNZQ4q7mM3r5WC2ll

Facebook link

https://www.facebook.com/AM-fashion-360192138160868/

Contact: 1) 9506918451 2) 8318070920

PEN AND LAPTOP

Instagram Handle:
@pen_and_laptop

Started On:
June 15,2020

Pen and Laptop is an Instagram handle of an aspiring writer. The page is dedicated to short stories, poems, quotes, reviews. The writer has managed to get a place in the blogs by Delhi Poetry Slam, some anthologies, and magazines. With the view that "Every creation is worth writing about" one can visit the page for soulful write-ups.

Email id: penandlaptop@gmail.com

ABOUT
FAMIAN PUBLISHERS

FAMIAN is an official online writing as well as publishing firm. It is the sky for Young Writers where they can unfurl their wings and can fly in their own arena. It is a platform to boost up the power of imagination of every author which they actually had never imagined.

FAMIAN is not just a platform and firm to express but also a station for encouragement, enthusiasm and improvement.

Today, where every digital-social interaction counts, it tries to do its best by making every interaction more inspirational. Famian is registered as a Government recognized startup on 31st May 2019.

You can reach FAMIAN at:

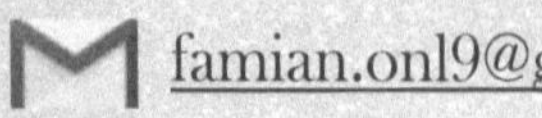 famian.onl9@gmail.com

 @famian.31

 https://www.facebook.com/famian.31/

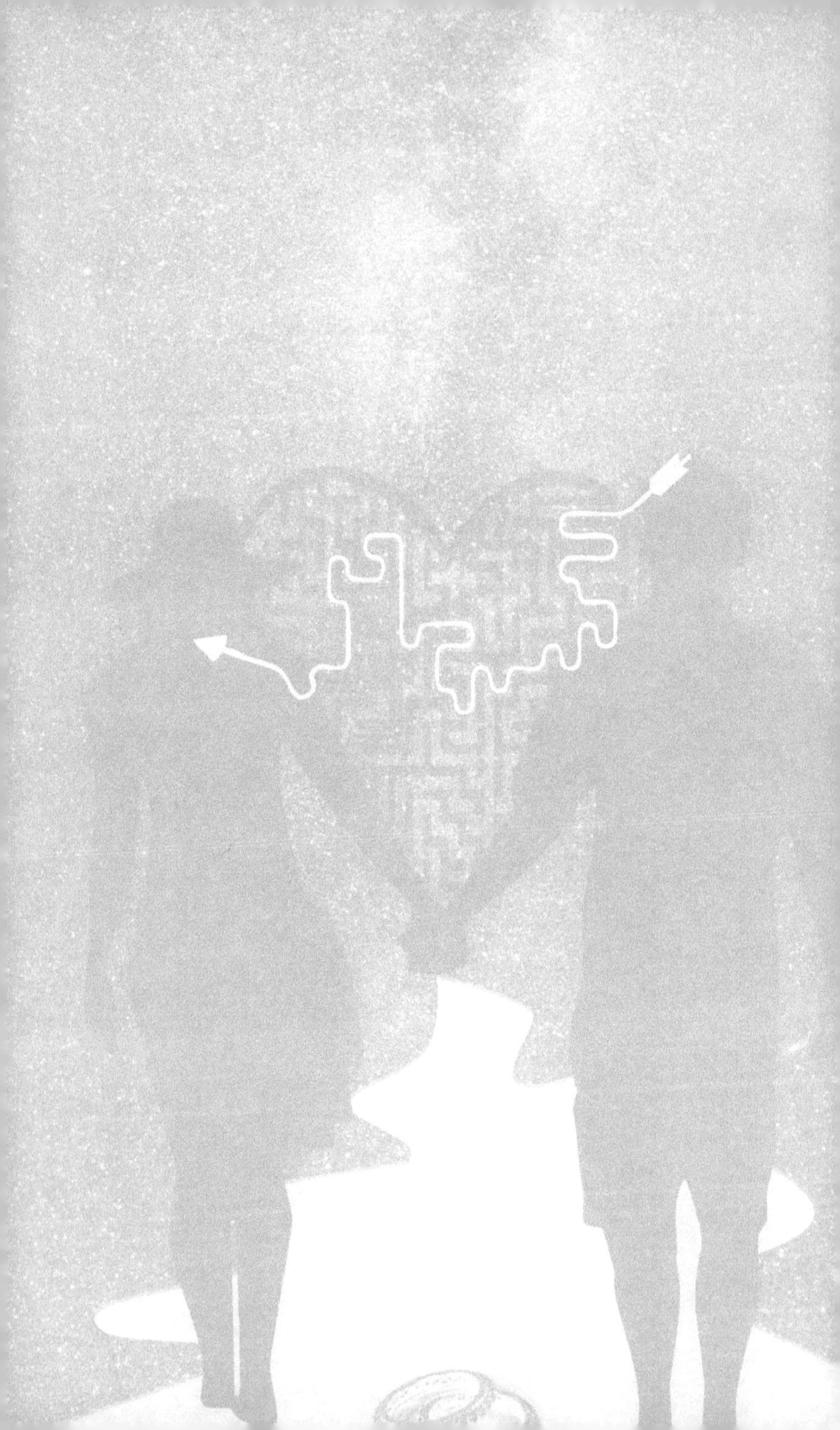

9 788194 953241